Royal Park Guides

The Regent's Park & Primrose Hill

Contents

Editor: Jeremy Harwood
Text: David MacFadyen
Design and illustration: Dennis Sterne

First published in Great Britain in 1999 by Essential Books Limited
7 Stucley Place, London NW1 8NS

A catalogue record for this book is available from the British Library.

ISBN: 1-902963-00-8

Of all the capital's Royal Parks, the park named after the eldest son of George III is the one that is most deeply woven into the heart of the city. It is an integral part of a grand design that reaches all the way down Portland Place and Regent Street to Piccadilly Circus and St James's, and therefore imparts, despite its rolling green acres, an air of urban sophistication unmatched by its rivals. The park's terraces and villas, mirrored in its lake, were a daring exercise in town planning intended to impress the rich and famous, while the Broad Walk, as originally conceived, was designed as a triumphal access way leading to a magnificent summer palace.

A royal hunting ground

The story of what is now the Regent's Park stretches much further back into the past. Once it was a part of the vast Forest of Middlesex, but, around the time of the Norman Conquest, the area was hived off to form the Manor of Tyburn, which, for the remainder of the Middle Ages, belonged to the Abbessess of Barking. After the Dissolution of the Monasteries, however, the land was appropriated by Henry VIII and, as Marylebone Park, it became a prized royal hunting preserve.

In 1645, at the height of the Civil War, Charles I was forced to mortgage the land to two of his supporters in return for cash to buy arms and munitions for his troops and, following his execution in 1649, the park, in common with all the Royal estates, was confiscated by Parliament. It was sold to speculators who, so it was reported, cut down 16,297 trees for quick profit before splitting the land up into smallholdings and letting these out to various tenant farmers. Although the monarchy

reclaimed ownership at the Restoration, the letting-out continued, the last person to hold the lease being the Duke of Portland, whose sub-tenants were farming the land at the start of the 1800s.

The Prince and the architect

By this time, the city was spreading northward and was almost touching what is now Marylebone Road on the park's southern boundary. It was clear that when the Duke of Portland's lease came up for renewal in 1811, there would be a splendid opportunity for the Crown itself to participate in the expansion and to reap a considerable profit as its reward. Accordingly, plans were sought for the development of the park area and for a street running to link it with fashionable St James's and Westminster.

The hour brought forth the man when John Nash became the Prince Regent's chosen architect. Regent Street was the backbone of Nash's scheme and the brilliant Quadrant (or quarter circle) at its bottom end,

was designed to throw the street on to a different axis, neatly separating seedy Soho from aristocratic Mayfair by a barricade of shops. Farther up, the round portico of All Souls, Langham Place, was intended to emphasize another curve, while the park itself was to be accessed by way of a terraced circus. From this, a wide avenue, now the Broad Walk, would lead to the Prince's palace at the north end of the park. All around the perimeter, noble terraces would look inward upon an idyllic landscape and an inner terraced circle, while the remainder of the space would be taken up by fifty-six villas, each set in its own splendid garden.

The uncompleted dream

Bankruptcies, changes of heart, and the turning of the Prince's mind to other projects all led to considerable alterations and truncation. In the end, only eight villas were ever built, while the Prince's summer palace never saw the light of day. The circus at the entrance became a crescent and a

Though much of the original scheme was never realized, the spirit of contributing to the mainstream of London life remained. The Zoo, the first of its kind in the world, was opened in 1827, and the gardens of the Royal Botanic Society – now Queen Mary's Gardens – a few years later. They continue to delight both Londoners and visitors alike, as do more recent additions, such as the Open Air Theatre, the superb display of roses in the Rose Garden, the exotic waterfowl on the Boating Lake and the thoughtfully refurbished gardens that provide a quiet haven of peace. At last, too, the park's somewhat theatrical architecture has also come to be cherished.

John Nash (top) and a section of his 1812 plan for the park (below).

square, while the site of the inner terraced circus was let as a garden to the Royal Botanical Society. The Zoological Society leased the north-east corner of the park, where Decimus Burton, Nash's friend and protégé, was commissioned to build a zoological garden. His notion of exhibiting the animals not simply in cages, but in attractive buildings set in a landscape, was much admired and much copied, too, during the ensuing decades.

The Zoo, as it was affectionately known almost from the start, opened its doors to the public in 1827. More and more sections of the park followed, starting with the formal Italian-style gardens inspired by the Prince Consort at the southern end of the Broad Walk, the site of today's Avenue Gardens. Despite a spirited rearguard action by the residents, most of it, including Primrose Hill, was open to the public by 1841. The process naturally discouraged further building and the public were also anxious that the open landscape should be retained.

The modern park

Though a Marylebone address held little appeal for the aristocracy, who usually preferred Mayfair and Belgravia, the new development became a magnet for the rich tradespeople of the West End, as well as for actors, writers and musicians. Many of these remained faithful even through the Victorian and the Edwardian eras, when Nash's work attracted more sneers than praise.

Ironically, it was the Second World War, when the park suffered greatly from bombs and neglect, that resulted in Nash's reputation being reinstated. Given the state of the park's crumpled buildings after the war, it was quickly recognized that there were only two courses of action open, either total demolition or total restoration. Fortunately, the latter was chosen. Today, even if the gleaming bastions of Nash's terraces now conceal offices and institutions, they still suggest the 'one entire Park compleat in unity of character' that was his inspiration back in the heady Regency days.

INNER CIRCLE

TRITON
FOUNTAIN

THEATRE

QUEEN MARY'S
GARDENS

ROSE
GARDEN

BEGONIA GARDEN

park
café

park
café

INNER CIRCLE

 Children's playground

 Toilets for the disabled

 Toilets

 Information

 Police

 Cafés & Refreshments
park
café

The overall plan of the park (right) shows its major features, internal and external access routes, and most convenient Underground stations. The detail (above) shows Queen Mary's Gardens within the Inner Circle.

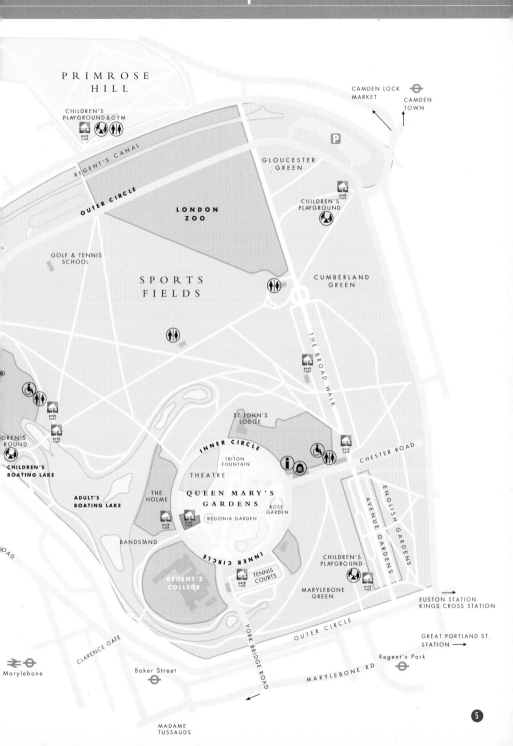

PRIMROSE HILL

CHILDREN'S PLAYGROUND & GYM

REGENT'S CANAL

OUTER CIRCLE

GLOUCESTER GREEN

CAMDEN LOCK MARKET

CAMDEN TOWN

LONDON ZOO

CHILDREN'S PLAYGROUND

GOLF & TENNIS SCHOOL

SPORTS FIELDS

CUMBERLAND GREEN

THE BROAD WALK

ST JOHN'S LODGE

INNER CIRCLE

TRITON FOUNTAIN

CHESTER ROAD

THEATRE

ENGLISH GARDENS

AVENUE GARDENS

DREN'S ROUND

CHILDREN'S BOATING LAKE

ADULT'S BOATING LAKE

THE HOLME

QUEEN MARY'S GARDENS

ROSE GARDEN

BEGONIA GARDEN

BANDSTAND

INNER CIRCLE

CHILDREN'S PLAYGROUND

REGENT'S COLLEGE

TENNIS COURTS

MARYLEBONE GREEN

EUSTON STATION KINGS CROSS STATION

GREAT PORTLAND ST. STATION

Regent's Park

CLARENCE GATE

OUTER CIRCLE

Marylebone

YORK BRIDGE ROAD

Baker Street

MARYLEBONE RD

MADAME TUSSAUDS

How long will it take?

You should allow at least an hour for this walk, assuming that you are proceeding at strolling pace, and longer if you intend to study and appreciate the beauties of the restored Avenue Gardens close to the walk's start.

1hr

Originally intended to lead to the Prince Regent's proposed summer retreat, the Broad Walk and the Avenue Gardens are the main features of the first part of this walk, which provides an excellent introduction to the many varied attractions that The Regent's Park has to offer. Park Crescent and Square, where the walk starts, are a triumph of early Regency style, and are among the most gracious elements of architect John Nash's original design. In contrast, the Italianate gardens are sumptuously high Victorian in flavour. The design and planting schemes here are based on the ones devised in 1861 at the behest of the Prince Consort by William Andrews Nesfield to replace the eight rows of trees – four to each side – that were Nash's contribution.

Comfort stops

park café

There are lavatories with disabled access at the start of the walk to the left of the Avenue Gardens by the entrance to the Broad Walk proper, and to the right at the entrance to Primrose Hill. An international selection of refreshments is available at the Broad Walk Park Café.

Look out for

The limes and tulip trees that line the inner and outer avenues of the Avenue Gardens, restored Victorian-style plantings based on Nesfield's original plans and the contrasting backdrop of the English garden. See, too, the curious Ready Money fountain and the panorama of notable buildings that you can spot across the city from the viewpoint on Primrose Hill.

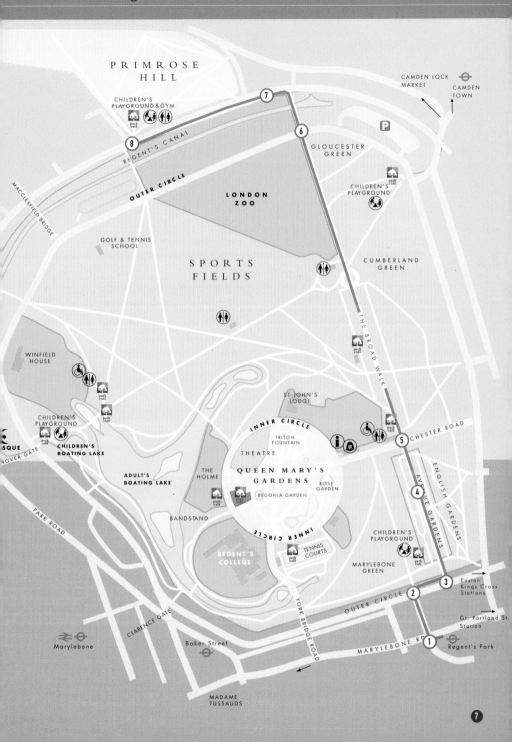

The Broad Walk and Primrose Hill

The elegantly Italianate Avenue Gardens (left) were the brainchild of the Prince Consort. They have now been restored to their full Victorian glory. One of their many ornamental features is the Lion Tazza (right).

1. Start the walk at elegant Park Crescent, by Regent's Park Underground station. Here, Nash's stylish rethinking of central London that stretches from Carlton House Terrace through Regent Street to Portland Place pauses for a moment before advancing into the park. Nothing advertises the architect's sureness of touch better than the proportions of this graceful curve of pillared mansions.

2. Cross Marylebone Road to Park Square East, following this round to St Andrew's Gate.

3. Enter the park and take the path bearing left. This leads to the Broad Walk, a mile-long northward promenade. Nash intended it as a grand approach to a summer palace for the Prince Regent, his friend and patron. But the Prince lost interest and the Walk leads instead to the Zoo and the Regent's Canal.

Improving on the Victorians, some of the Avenue Gardens' elaborate ornamental structures are now eye-catching fountains (below).

Walk Commentary

4. Strong features of Nesfield's design were formal, but colourful, plantings of spring bulbs and summer bedding, tiered fountains, evergreen hedges to give year-round form, and vast stone urns and tazzas – ornamental bowls – filled with flowers. Two World Wars and years of decay took their toll, and it was not until 1993, by which time

only about half of the original layout remained intact, that a major restoration programme got under way. This was much aided by the rediscovery of Nesfield's planting plans and catalogues, and by the survival of some of the original artificial stone features. These provided the patterns from which others could be made. Today, the garden is much as the Victorians would have known it. In their Italianate

4. The first section of the Broad Walk to Chester Road houses the Avenue Gardens. Planting and design schemes, devised by the Victorian horticulturalist William Andrews Nesfield, have now been restored to their full glory, aided by the rediscovery of his plans and catalogues, and by the survival of some of the artificial stone features. The Lion Tazza, a massive ornamental bowl at the centre of the gardens, is an original.

The Ready Money fountain (left) was out of use for many years before it was restored to full working order. At the same time, the surrounding landscape was given back its Victorian character (sketch, below).

Complementing this is the informal English garden of orchards and spring meadows that Nesfield's son, Markham, added to the area between the Avenue Gardens and the Outer Circle.

5. Cross the Chester Road and enter the Broad Walk proper. The Walk here is an

surroundings, the fountains, which are a modern touch, splash and sparkle, while the formal plantings are bounded by low hedges of box and lavender, punctuated by mopheaded hollies and slim conifers. And, once again, the massive Lion Tazza and the other urns, bowls and vases down the garden's length are awash with seasonal colours.

5. The ornate Gothic Ready Money

drinking fountain at the end of the Broad Walk was erected in 1869, its construction paid for by the memorably named Sir Cowasjee Jehangir Ready-Money. A wealthy Parsee from Bombay, he made the gift, as the inscription on the fountain testifies, 'as a token of gratitude to the people of England for the protection enjoyed by him and his Parsee fellow countrymen under the British rule in India'.

6. The Regent's Canal was originally intended by Nash as a commercial venture – he and his wife held the majority of the shares in the company that built and ran it. Only a

Painted narrow-
boats ply back and
forth along the
quiet waters of the
Regent's Canal
(left) from Camden
Lock in the east to
Little Venice to the
west.

avenue with a belt of trees on either side. Through them and across a wide expanse of grass to the right are distant views of the white cliffs of the Nash terraces, while on the left are playing fields. Also on the left is the black-and-white Broad Walk café. Ahead, look out for the Gothic pinnacles and patterning of the oddly-named Ready Money fountain, erected by the grandly-titled Metropolitan Drinking Fountain and Cattle

Trough Association in 1869. Beyond, behind a stout wire face, are some of the Zoo buildings, founded by Sir Stamford Raffles and the Zoological Society of London in 1826. Sometimes animals can be glimpsed, while generally there is a pink blaze of flamingoes ready to catch the eye.

6. At St Mark's Gate, cross the Outer Circle and then take St Mark's Bridge across the Regent's Canal. Below the bridge, in Cumberland

Basin, traditional narrow-boats, bright with paint and baskets of flowers, lie moored. It is well worth considering taking a water-bus ride along the canal itself, as this will give you a fine view of both park and zoo. The service runs between Camden Lock and Little Venice. Alternatively, make a short detour along the towpath before return-ing to St Mark's bridge.

7. Turn left along Prince Albert Road to the traffic

Traditional China meets
Regency London along
the Regent's Canal
where this floating
restaurant-junk (right)
is moored.

generation later, falling revenues meant that it narrowly missed being filled in to provide a new railway line. It is now one of the Park's most attractive hidden features.

7. Primrose Hill is a sloping mead-ow dotted with plane and hawthorn trees, and with pretty cast-iron lamp posts. Duels and murder feature in its history, while the medieval seer Mother Shipton prophesized that if ever London grew big enough to surround it, the streets of the city would run with blood. More prosaically, it was bought from Eton

'Jumbo' (left) meets his fans in the Zoo, opened in 1827 and the first of its kind in the world. Even today, animals can be glimpsed – and heard – from within the park.

lights by the Zoo exit and cross over to the gate into Primrose Hill. This is on the corner of Albert Terrace, an attractive collection of substantial early 19th-century houses clad in blue, cream, fawn or pink plaster. On one of them, a blue plaque announces that it was the home of Roger Fenton, the great 19th-century photographic pioneer.

8. Take the path that climbs the hill straight in front of you to reach the viewpoint.

Once you get to the top, you will see that the view to the foreground is dominated by the Zoo, with the cylinders of Sir Hugh Casson's Elephant House and Lord Snowdon's geometric Aviary clearly visible. But the greatest attraction is the infinitely variegated skyline of London itself, from Canary Wharf and the Millennium Dome in the east to the Post Office Tower and beyond. You can get a clear view of every lofty pinnacle

of church, state and commerce, with an indicator close by on the hilltop to help you identify them.

9. From Primrose Hill, follow the signs to Chalk Farm Underground station.

The 18th-century view from Primrose Hill before London grew up around it. (right).

College in 1841 and opened to the public to pacify the ordinary folk, who were then denied access to parts of Regent's Park. It has been a favourite leisure venue ever since.

How long will it take?

The time this walk takes can easily expand into the time you have available. If you intend to explore Queen Mary's Gardens fully, the Rose Garden and the Begonia Garden being specific stopping-off points, you should allow at least an hour, and more if you continue on to St John's Lodge Garden.

1hr

Though this walk looks short, allow plenty of time for it, since there is simply so much to see and absorb, especially if you are a keen gardener. Within the Inner Circle lies one of the park's chief glories — Queen Mary's Gardens. Officially, these date from the 1935 Royal Jubilee when, as the massive gilded gates at the entrance testify, the gardens were renamed in honour of George V's consort, Queen Mary, but in fact, gardening here has a much longer history. From 1838 to 1930, this was the home of the Royal Botanic Society's gardens, the centrepiece of which was a huge conservatory that could hold 2,000 at a time. In the end, the Society was defeated by rising costs, the gardens taken over by the park and the conservatory demolished. There is so much that is unmissable here: perhaps the greatest treat for both eye and nose is the magnificent rose garden.

Comfort stops

park café

There are lavatories to the right on York Bridge, beyond the crossing over the Boating Lake, and just further on to the right, the Park Café by the Tennis Centre. Inside Queen Mary's Gardens is the Rose Garden Park Café, while there are more lavatories with disabled access just down from the Chester Road entry point.

Look out for

The Rose Garden, the rare Euodia between a large plane tree and the Lombardy Poplars that partially surround the Begonia Garden, the Begonia Garden itself, the bronzes and shield-bearing cherubs in the gardens of St John's Lodge, the Yoshino Cherries and the Triton Fountain, and the view of The Holme.

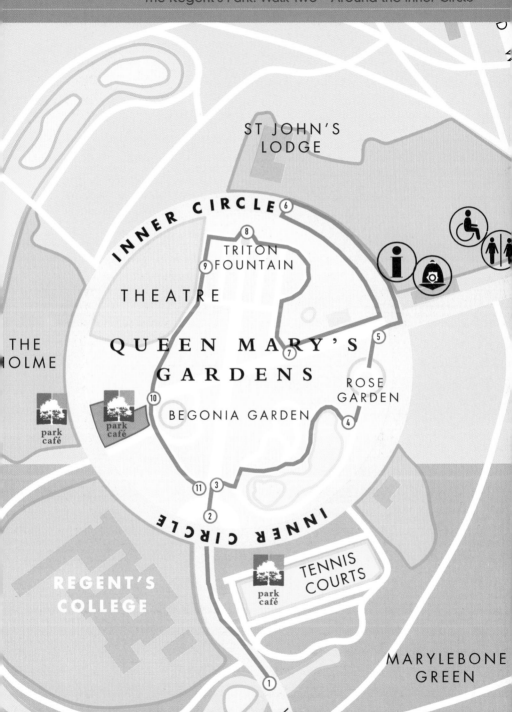

ST JOHN'S
LODGE

INNER CIRCLE ⑥

⑧

⑨ TRITON
FOUNTAIN

THEATRE

THE
OLME

QUEEN MARY'S
GARDENS

⑤

⑦

ROSE
GARDEN

⑩

BEGONIA GARDEN

④

park
café

park
café

⑪ ③

②

INNER CIRCLE

REGENT'S
COLLEGE

park
café

TENNIS
COURTS

①

MARYLEBONE
GREEN

YOR

UTER

⑬

The magnificent gates to Queen Mary's Gardens (left), erected to commemorate the 1935 Royal Jubilee, are a powerful reminder of the great days of empire.

park by Sigismund Goetze, a wealthy, successful artist and local resident, who was one of the park's most generous benefactors between the World Wars. Opposite, to the left, lies Regent's College. Formerly Bedford College, it was the first educational establishment to provide university education for women.

1. Enter the Inner Circle via York Gate, York Terrace and York Bridge. The nearest Underground station is Baker Street. Walk along Marylebone Road past Madame Tussauds and the Planetarium to reach York Gate.

2. The Jubilee Gates mark the entrance to Queen Mary's Gardens. They were donated to the

3. Go through the gates and turn right to the foot of the small, ornamental lake. Just beyond is an island

The formal-style Begonia Garden (right) is one of this walk's major attractions. It is located just by the Rose Garden Park Café.

The striking Japanese–style eagle (right) is a dominant feature on the little island at the southern end of the lake. Outlined by swagged pillars, over which ramblers and climbing roses scramble, the neatly squared beds within the Rose Garden (below) are home to practically every kind of rose imaginable, from modern cultivars to traditional old–fashioneds.

impression being completed by the cascading willows that dimple the water with their leaves.

4. At the head of the lake, on the left is **The Lost Bow**, a charming little bronze, and beyond, the Rose Garden.

5. Bear left from the Rose Garden and proceed until you reach the Chester Road gateway. Go through and turn left along the Inner Circle.

composed of rough stone blocks covered with alpines and rock plants, and decorated with a tall stone lantern and, at the far side, a dramatically-plunging Japanese bronze eagle. An arched Chinese-style footbridge links the island to the shore, the oriental

---

4. The Rose Garden houses one of the finest collections of roses in the country, with an estimated 30,000 plants representing nearly 400 varieties. Species, old roses, floribundas, hybrid teas and modern shrubs are among the roses that make up the displays. Swags of rambler roses hang between tall pillars that are themselves practically swamped by climbers, encircling bed upon bed of more formal plantings, featuring large- and cluster-flowered varieties.

6. The path to the garden is arched by a pergola on which clematis and roses climb. At its end, is an urn on a plinth, a memorial to the journalist Anne Sharpley. Beyond is the garden. An immaculate sunken lawn, with a stone pier at each corner, forms the Lodge's forecourt. Each pier is decorated with a cherub bearing a shield on which are emblazoned the arms of the Bute family – a reminder that the garden was commissioned by the third Marquess as a place 'fit for meditation'. Opposite, through alleys of clipped yew, is another wide lawn.

Henry Pegram's **Hylas and the Nymph**, presented to the park in 1933, is one of the most striking ornaments of the 'secret garden' at St John's Lodge.

The artificial cascade in Queen Mary's Gardens brings a dramatically Alpine touch to the park scene.

6. Opposite is a police station, the park nurseries and, just beyond, St John's Lodge. Part of Nash's original scheme, this was one of the first villas to be completed in the park. It has been much enlarged and altered over the years and now, with its cupolas, urns, decorations and coating of pure white plaster, it has the air of a huge, delicious wedding cake. Though the house is closed to the public, its garden is open, although the access is so discreetly concealed that the place is often called the 'secret garden'. Look for the signs that mark its entrance.

7. Return to the Chester Road gateway and, once inside Queen Mary's Gardens, take the first path to the right. Follow the yew hedge around to a musical little cascade falling into a woodland pool. Nearby are fossilized tree stumps brought to the site from Dorset in 1845.

8. At the junction with the main avenue, you will see the Triton Fountain, with the Jubilee Gates at the avenue's far end.

9. Continue around the sidepath, following the line of hedges, and then bear left to reach the Open Air Theatre. Now one of London's established summer institutions, it was no more than a grassy mound with deckchairs when it opened in 1932, a far cry from the thousand-seater

The Goatherd's Daughter (left) is dedicated 'to all protectors of the defenceless'.

garden rooms, with low walls of clipped lavender or box. They encompass small knot gardens and other planting schemes.

surrounded by herbaceous borders and massed roses with, as its centrepiece, a large bronze group of Hylas and the Nymph standing in a stone-rimmed pool. Nearby is another delightful bronze, The Goatherd's Daughter, erected by the National Council for Animal Welfare.

7. As you walk, you will observe what is really a series of small

8. The Triton Fountain itself dates from 1950. It is an impressive work, complete with a merman who holds a conch shell while he and his accompanying mermaids simultaneously spout water at the park. An inscription on its stone rim says that the fountain was presented to the park in memory of Sigismund Goetze, who donated many of the gardens' features.

The Open Air Theatre's summer schedule usually includes a Shakespearean play and a musical. The scenes (left, below) are from A Midsummer Night's Dream.

theatre it has now become. Every summer it presents at least three productions.

10. Continue parallel to the Inner Circle, across which you can see The Holme, another picture-postcard villa from the park's Regency beginnings and one of the few to be built. It was designed by the 18-year-old Decimus Burton for his father, which may account for the building's exuberant frontage. Immediately to hand is the Rose Garden Park Café, a pleasant series of glass octagons, which faces the bright and colourful bedding of the Begonia Garden. This has a contemplative bronze, the Boy and Frog, by Sir William Read Dick in its midst.

11. Leave the park the way you came via the Jubilee Gates and York Gate, or walk around the Outer Circle to Park Square Gardens for Regent's Park Underground station.

The Boy and Frog (right), a feature of the Begonia Garden, was donated to the park in 1936. It was another gift from philanthropist Sigismund Goetze, one of Regent's Park's most substantial modern benefactors.

How long will it take?

The full walk, without stopping, takes around forty minutes, but you should allow at least an hour so that you can take in a visit to the Nature Study and Waterfowl Care Centre and enjoy the lake's bird-watching facilities.

40 mins

Though much of John Nash's vision for The Regent's Park was never realized, it is probably on this walk that you can catch the best glimpse of what he had in mind. The 9-hectare (22-acre), Y-shaped lake is the walk's centrepiece. With its six islands, it is still just as Nash planned it, giving the scene the atmosphere of a rural retreat in the heart of the pounding city. So, too, is what lies opposite – a building scheme of elegant, classical design to complement the perfection of the landscape. Facing inward upon the lake are the columns and pediments of the stylish terraces Nash so lovingly created, and, reflected in the water, the icing-sugar perfection of the villas conceived as an integral part of the overall scheme.

Comfort stops

park café

There is a refreshment kiosk and lavatories with disabled access located just across Hanover Bridge, which spans the lake towards its eastern end, the Rose Garden Park Café in Queen Mary's Gardens, and lavatories and the Park Café at the Tennis Centre off York Bridge Road.

Look out for

The herons that nest on the island known as the Heronry, the weeping willows, White and Silver Willows, poplars and alders along the edge of the lake, and the view of The Holme, the only villa by the lakeside. Just before York Bridge, note the large Crack Willow and Common Hornbeam immediately inside the boundary fence of Regent's College.

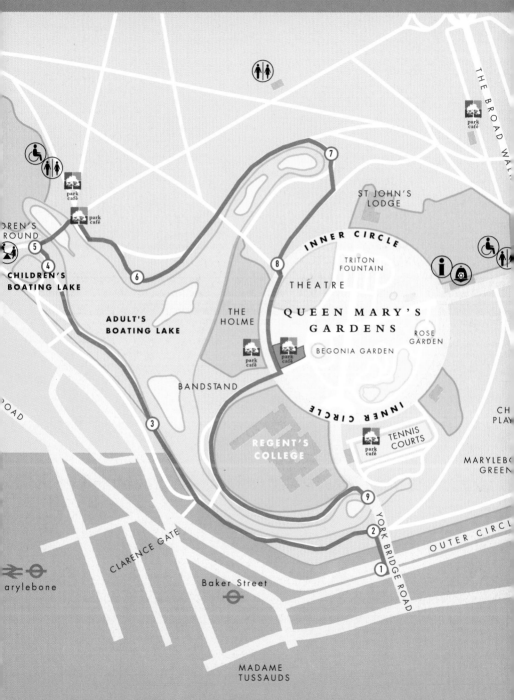

THE BROAD WALK

park café

ST JOHN'S
LODGE

INNER CIRCLE

TRITON
FOUNTAIN

THÉATRE

QUEEN MARY'S
GARDENS

ROSE
GARDEN

BEGONIA GARDEN

THE
HOLME

park café

park café

INNER CIRCLE

BANDSTAND

TENNIS
COURTS

park café

REGENT'S
COLLEGE

CH
PLAY

MARYLEBO
GREEN

park café

park café

CHILDREN'S
BOATING LAKE

ADULT'S
BOATING LAKE

REN'S
ROUND

OAD

CLARENCE GATE

Baker Street

arylebone

YORK BRIDGE ROAD

OUTER CIRCL

MADAME
TUSSAUDS

The Boating Lake and Beyond

York Bridge (right) provides an elegant access way to the attractions of the Boating Lake. One of them is the herons that nest on the first of the lake's six islands (left).

On the other side of York Bridge Road is Marylebone Green. This is the location for the recently refounded Regent's Park Flower Show, held annually in June, which revives the splendour of the 19th-century flower shows in the park for a modern popular audience.

1. Enter the park by York Gate, a short distance from Baker Street Underground station. Behind is the pale, pillared bank of York Terrace, divided into two to present a view of St Marylebone parish church.

2. Walk down to the lake, turn left and follow the lake-side path until you are opposite the first of the lake's six islands. This is the Heronry, established by the birds themselves. The herons began nesting on the island in the late 1960s, and there are now at least twenty-five breeding pairs, whose untidy nests can be seen high in the trees.

3. Continue up the side of the lake. This is, in fact, the River Tyburn, which rises in Hampstead Heath and flows to the Thames. Nash dammed its waters to feed both this lake and the smaller one in Queen Mary's Gardens. These are

Walk Commentary

1. The arched tower that peers over the trees is that of the Abbey National building that stands on the site of 221b Baker Street, home of Sir Arthur Conan Doyle's immortal detective Sherlock Homes. York Gate itself dates from 1822 and its stylish elegance drew some celebrated residents, including the Victorian actor-manager William Macready and Frances Palgrave, compiler of the 'Golden Treasury of Poetry'.

Millions have taken pleasure in the Boating Lake (above) since Nash's time, whether walking or resting by its shores, or rowing on its waters.

Regent's Park has been a sanctuary for waterfowl and a stopping-off place for migrants almost since its beginnings. This watercolour of waterfowl by Hanover Island (right) was painted in 1880.

the only points where the Tyburn emerges into the open, the rest of its journey being underground. On the left, note the curious pointed domes of Sussex Place and, on the far side of the lake, The Holme, the first villa to be completed in the park.

4. Keep on to the end of this spur of the lake, where you will find a children's boating pond. Here, canoes, rowing boats and pedallos can be hired for the over-5's. There is also a playground with a sandpit, slides and swings.

5. From the boating pond, turn right over Longbridge, where an authentic-looking cataract foams into the lake. Across the bridge, next to the lavatories, you will find the Nature Study and Waterfowl Care Centre. This features an Information Room, where visitors can find out more about the park's wildlife, but only small groups can be admitted at any one time. On the opposite bank, there is a new boat hiring facility, opening in spring 2000, with catering attached. The present facility closes in October 1999.

6. Follow the path around the next arm of the lake, which has a chain stretched across it to bar access to rowing boats. This is to provide safe areas for waterfowl, of which there are many in the vicinity. Carry on past the next

The Royal Waterfowl Collection actively encourages the birds of the lake to breed. Note the convenient ramps that encourage access from the water to these duck nesting boxes (right).

2. In or by the lake, you can spot all sorts of unfamiliar wildfowl. You may catch a glimpse of black, black-necked and whooper swans, with their black and yellow beaks, bean, bar-headed, white-fronted, Hawaiian and Canada geese (the former once almost extinct in the wild), plus seemingly innumerable vividly-plumed ducks. The birds are all part

The Boating Lake and Beyond

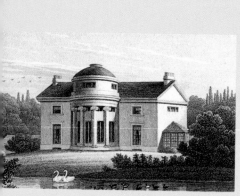

The Holme (not open to the public) was built in around 1818 by James Burton to a design by his 18-year-old son, Decimus (right). Its Corinthian portico and bay front are perhaps a little too elaborate for the house's size (above).

bridge to the island, on which nesting boxes and feeders make it clear that smaller birds are also well-catered for. A recognition guide is displayed to help you identify the various species. Farther along, on the next island, are carefully-graded nesting boxes for ducks of various sizes.

7. Follow the curve of the lake around. Ahead, on the far side of a prairie of a playing field, the peaks of London Zoo's famous

cliff-like Mappin Terraces are clearly visible. Once around the curve, look out for the gracious rear elevation of St John's Lodge, a contemporary of The Holme. A glimpse of the Post Office Tower makes an odd contrast to this.

8. Continue to the Inner Circle and turn right. Opposite is the stage door of the Open Air Theatre and on the right, the ornamental gates and red drive of The Holme, whose gardens run down to the lakeside at this point. When you reach

A Great Crested Grebe (right), just one of the park's many bird visitors.

of the park's Royal Waterfowl Collection, started during Queen Victoria's reign and now embracing almost seventy species. There is a helpful identification chart on display at Longbridge.

3. From kestrels to grebes, many other unusual city-dwellers have made their homes in the park. Over the last twenty years, more than 150 species of birds have been recorded

St John's Lodge, as originally conceived in all its elegance (left). Only the gardens are now open to the public (see Walk Two).

Queen Mary's Gardens, go right down the path opposite, back into the park and towards the lake. You pass neatly-clipped hedges and colourful rows of bedding plants until, by the water, you reach a pretty Victorian bandstand, backed by willows. A plaque commemorates the army bandsmen killed there in an IRA bomb attack. Concerts are given here in summer.

9. Continue on the path as it follows the outer boundary of the grounds of Regent's College and on to York Gate, where you turn right for the return to Baker Street Underground station.

Skating on the lake was a popular Victorian recreation (right). The water level was lowered after the ice gave way in 1867 and more than forty drowned.

there, some flying in from as far away as Siberia. Part of the reason for this popularity is that birds migrating over London tend to fly from one watering place to another, following a south-westerly line in autumn and a north-easterly one in winter. Regent's Park lies right in the middle of both routes and has the added attraction of London Zoo and its leftover animal foodstuffs.

Having had the better part of two centuries to think things over, Londoners have at last conceived a deep affection for the park's Outer Circle. This was by far from always being the case. When its terraces and buildings were first erected, many people thought them slipshod in style, when compared to the rigid classicism that was the architectural norm of the day. Victorian taste, on the other hand, found them showy and dishonest, in that the palatial frontages on to the park were merely masks to disguise the terraced rows of somewhat lesser houses behind them. It was also suspected, at the time, that the universal coatings of cream or fawn stucco that had been so liberally applied might be concealing a good deal of jerry-building.

Whatever the rights and wrongs, it is really in its collective grandeur that the glory of the Outer Circle lies. An exploration of it gives you a very particular glimpse into the character of the capital. With its mighty pediments bristling with allegorical statuary, its triumphal arches and massive porticos, its caryatids and forests of columns, it resembles a setting fit for the grandest of operas, or an imaginary classical cityscape rendered on some vast canvas by a Romantic master-painter. Some of the detail, too, is delightful, from dummy windows and a runic inscription to cast-iron street furniture that still bears the royal cipher of George IV. It is a rich backdrop that makes its own contribution to the park's glamour.

Sussex Place (above) and Park Crescent (right) are examples of Nash's Outer Circle vision at its most penetrating.

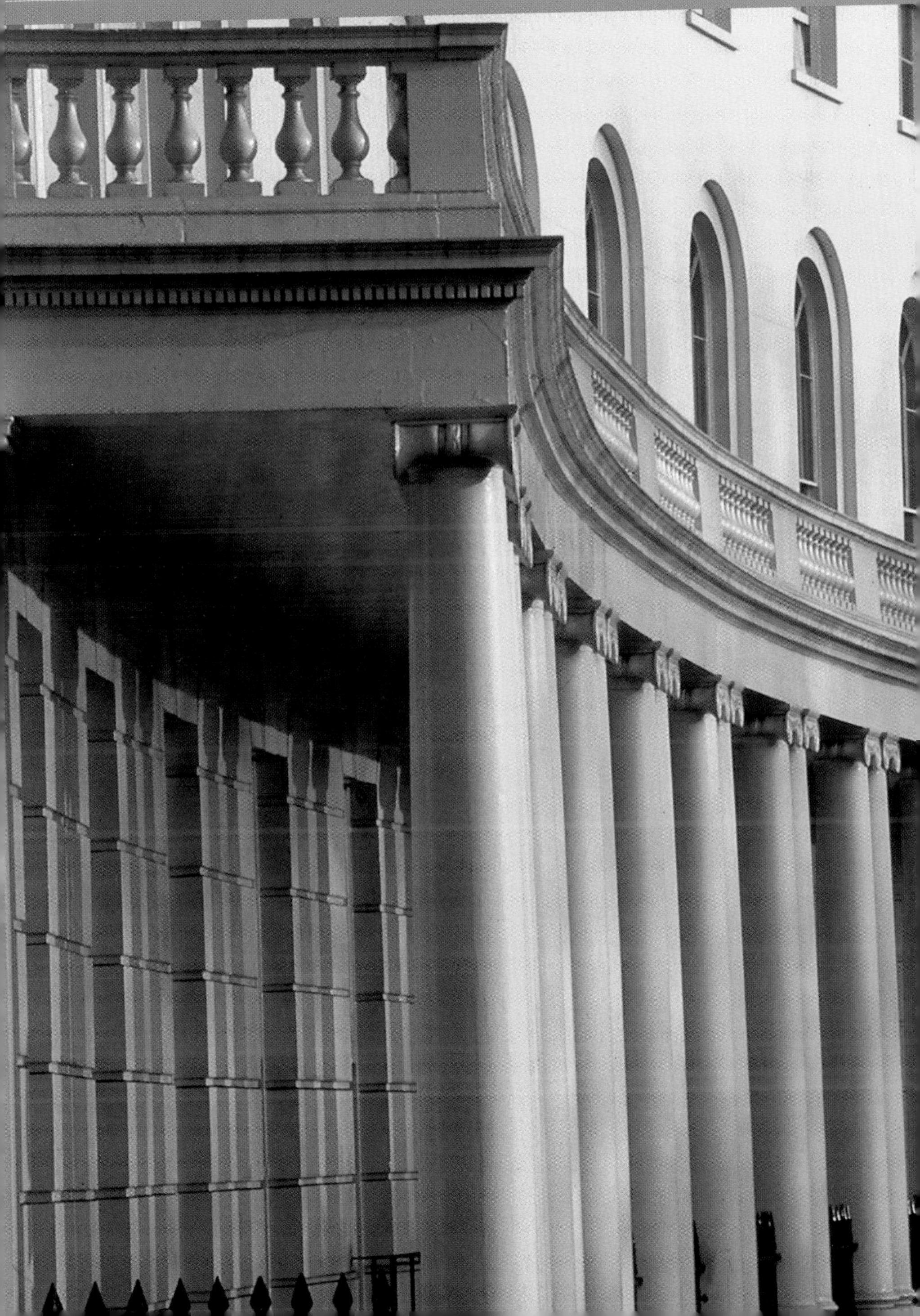

How long will it take?

To walk around the whole of the Outer Circle takes a good hour and a half, which is why it may be an option to cut short the walk at Gloucester Gate. To do this, leave the park via Parkway for Camden Town Underground station, which is close at hand, as are the attractions of Camden Lock, which is also the starting point for narrow-boat trips down Regent's Park Canal.

Comfort stops

park café

There are lavatories for children at Marylebone Green and, again for children, at Gloucester Green, where there is a Park Café kiosk in the children's playground. Car parking along the Outer Circle is pay-and-display, note the scheme continues to operate on Sundays. There is also parking at Gloucester Slips.

Look out for

The plane tree outside the Royal College of Physicians in St Andrew's Place which, so it is said, is a direct descendant of the tree on the Greek island of Cos, under which the ancient medical sage, Hippocrates taught, Park Village for its charming architecture, the Jelling Stone, a copy of a Viking runic stone, in the garden of the Danish Church and also the Danish Church itself.

PRIMROSE
HILL

CHILDREN'S
PLAYGROUND & GYM

park
café

REGENT'S CANAL

CAMDEN LOCK
MARKET

CAMDEN
TOWN

P

GLOUCESTER
GREEN

OUTER CIRCLE

LONDON
ZOO

CHILDREN'S
PLAYGROUND

park
café

⑦

⑥

MACCLESFIELD BRIDGE

⑧

GOLF & TENNIS
SCHOOL

SPORTS
FIELDS

CUMBERLAND
GREEN

⑤

THE BROAD WALK

park
café

WINFIELD
HOUSE

park
café

park
café

ST JOHN'S
LODGE

park
café

CHESTER ROAD

④

CHILDREN'S
PLAYGROUND

park
café

CHILDREN'S
BOATING LAKE

⑩

·SQUE

OVER GATE

INNER CIRCLE

TRITON
FOUNTAIN

THEATRE

QUEEN MARY'S
GARDENS

THE
HOLME

ADULT'S
BOATING LAKE

ROSE
GARDEN

BEGONIA GARDEN

i

ENGLISH GARDENS

AVENUE GARDENS

③

park
café

park
café

BANDSTAND

INNER CIRCLE

⑪

PARK ROAD

REGENT'S
COLLEGE

park
café

TENNIS
COURTS

CHILDREN'S
PLAYGROUND

park
café

MARYLEBONE
GREEN

②

CLARENCE GATE

YORK BRIDGE ROAD

OUTER CIRCLE

①

Gt. Portland St.
Station

Marylebone

Baker Street

⑫

MARYLEBONE RD

Regent's Park

MADAME
TUSSAUDS

The Diorama (above) opened its doors to the public in 1823. Despite initial popularity, it failed to hold its audience and was eventually forced to close in 1848.

concrete and black brick headquarters of the Royal College of Physicians. This dates from the 1960s, when it ousted a Nash villa from the site. The new building was much admired at the time and is now a Grade 1 listed building, though purists might argue that its sharp, angular lines strike a slightly discordant note among all the Regency roundness.

intended to become another of the early park's great tourist attractions when he opened it in 1827. With a rotunda larger than the dome of St Paul's Cathedral, on which was painted an enormous panorama of the capital, it also housed a sculpture museum, a hall of mirrors and a cyclorama. Though initially popular, the success did not last, and eventually it was pulled down.

1. Start at Park Square, close to Regent's Park Underground station and with plenty of parking space. Built in the early 1820s, the square consists of two pale-stuccoed terraces facing each other across a fenced garden.

2. Turn right into the Outer Circle. Here, the cream porticos and bow windows of St Andrew's Terrace and Place gaze impassively upon the angular white

3. Continue on to Cambridge Gate. This is also something of a stranger, the more so because it is faced with gold-flecked Bath stone and not the otherwise universal stucco. Built in 1875, its lofty, slated towers make it look more like a Parisian hotel of the Grande Epoque, rather than a native of London. It took the place of The Colosseum, which Decimus Burton, its creator,

4. Chester Terrace lies a little farther to the north. This is Nash on the grandest of grand scales, with 300 yards and more of elegant gleaming cream stucco fronted by gigantic pillars and topped with statues of female goddesses and other deities. The huge balconied front seems almost purpose-planned by Nash as an imposing saluting base, while project-

The interior of the Colosseum under construction (above). It, too, failed and was eventually demolished.

Walk Commentary

1. The large central block, Park Square East, now occupied by The Prince's Trust, bears the large black superscription DIORAMA, with a commemorative plaque alongside. This is all that remains of Jacques Daguerre's Diorama, the forerunner of the cinema and one of London's greatest tourist attractions in its day. A rotating auditorium presented the spellbound audience with two distinct scenes, arranged within 'Picture Rooms', each considerably larger than the actual auditorium.

Performances lasted for fifteen minutes at a time. Suitably dramatic musical accompaniments heightened the atmosphere, as did spectacular trompe l'oeils.

2. The marker beneath a plane tree in the garden of the Royal College of Physicians claims that the tree is a direct descendant of the one on Cos, under which Hippocrates, one of medicine's founding fathers and originator of the Hippocratic Oath, is said to have taught. Whether this is true or not, the college itself was actually founded in 1518 and it is the

ing wings are linked to the main building by soaring triumphal arches bearing the terrace's name. However, there is a surprise in store. Despite the pomp, the front doors of the houses open on to a quiet, raised roadway, divided by a balustrade from a strip of garden and the main carriageway. Behind the terrace, reached through a Doric arch, is Chester Row North, rebuilt after Second World War bomb damage but mingling well with the more modest second tier of Regency terraces tucked away behind the flamboyant front row.

5. Neighbouring Cumberland Terrace is even more extravagant. Named, like the other terraces, after the titles of the mostly disreputable sons of George III, it is made up of three blocks linked by

decorated triumphal arches. The central block is topped by a massive pediment, within which huge allegorical sculptures cavort against a Wedgewood-blue background. The figures are said to represent Britannia and the arts, sciences and trade of her empire, but they may signify something else entirely.

6. Next to Cumberland Terrace is the Danish Church, with its delicate Gothic brick front. The church was built in 1826 to serve as the chapel for the neighbouring St Katherine's Hospital: it got its present name during the First World War when, at the request of

The view north across Cumberland Green looks towards Cumberland Terrace and what was to become the Danish Church (above). Nash was determined to place his buildings in the context of a countryside idyll.

the Danish-born Queen Alexandra, the widow of Edward VII, it became the official place of worship for Danes in London. The airy interior features 18th-century furnishings salvaged from the original chapel, which was situated on the banks of the Thames close to Tower Bridge, together with decorative flights of angels bearing the coats of arms of the hospital's royal benefactors throughout the centuries. In addition, the

oldest medical society in the whole country.

3. Cumberland Terrace is truly magnificent in outward appearance: in reality, it is an equally magnificent fake. After the Second World War, it was discovered that a combination of enemy action and cheap building materials had left the terrace in a sorry state. The entire rear was therefore demolished and new flats and houses erected behind the original facade. The eye-catching effect Nash intended still impresses with its sheer magnitude.

4. Outside the door of the Danish Church is a large stone covered with mysterious runic inscriptions. It is a copy of one set up at Jelling in Jutland in AD 980 by King Harald of Denmark, the grandson of King Canute, in memory of his parents and to commemorate that he 'had won all Norway and Denmark to himself and made the Danes Christians'.

5. Both sections of Park Village were part of Nash's scheme, but are quite unlike the grand edifices within the park itself. The houses, intended as

Cumberland Terrace (above) was named after the Duke of Cumberland, probably the most unpopular of George III's sons.

An unusual side view of Chester Terrace (right), featuring one of the street lamps that are, like much of the ornamental detail in the park, the subject of a government-preservation order.

church has fine wooden carvings of Moses and St John the Baptist by the 17th-century Danish sculptor Caius Cibber, while a model of a trading vessel hangs from the ceiling.

7. Gloucester Gate follows. Another Nash terrace, it is all creamy stucco, gigantic pilasters and yet more neo-classical sculptures, this time set against a terracotta backdrop. Beside it, the park's north-east gate leads out to Albany Street, on the other side of which can be seen Park Village West and the surviving half of Park Village East. The other half was obliterated by the coming of the railway.

8. Continue westward, towards and past London Zoo. The lack of buildings here is a deliberate omission, as the original intention was to provide terrace-dwellers with an uninterrupted view north to Highgate and Hampstead. Opposite the running track, on the left, lies the Golf and Tennis School: Edward VIII and Wallis Simpson both took refresher courses there before the crisis broke that was to lead to Edward's abdication.

9. Beyond to the left is Winfield House, the London residence of the United States ambassador. Buried in trees and lofty fencing, it stands on the site of St Dunstan's House, built in 1825 for the fabulously wealthy third Marquess of Hertford, widely known as the 'Caliph of Regent's Park' and the original for Thackeray's villainous Marquess of Steyne in Vanity Fair. The present house was the creation of Barbara Hutton, the Woolworth heiress, who bought St Dunstan's House in 1937, demolished it and put up the present neo-Georgian residence in its place. Opposite, on the left, are two delightful, richly decorated mock Regency cottages, Gothick Lodge and Ionic Lodge.

10. Proceed until you reach the London Central Mosque, with its golden copper dome and slender minaret. It stands in the grounds of what was North Villa and is now the Islamic

Gleaming white stucco characterized Nash's flamboyant building work around the park (left).

dwellings for the prosperous middle classes, are small, charming and built in a wide variety of styles — Gothic, cottagey, Italian, French and Swiss Chalet. Some, indeed, are two houses designed to look like one from the outside, an early venture into the semi-detached that was to considerably influence suburban architecture for a century to come.

The slender minaret of the London Central Mosque (above), a magnet for the city's Islamic community.

Cultural Centre. The mosque itself – a focal point for the city's Islamic community – dates from 1978 but, in part, owes its existence to funds raised by the Nizam of Hyderabad half a century earlier. Its plain, dignified and spacious interior is illuminated by a magnificent chandelier, while the walls are inscribed with quotations from the Koran.

11. Hanover Terrace, designed by Nash in

classical mode, consists of twenty houses linked by an arcade along the ground floor, and by pillars between the first and second floors at the centre. Porticoes crowned with statuary at either end balance the whole. Sussex Place, by comparison, looks positively skittish, with curved wings, tall bow windows and no fewer than ten octagonal, pointed cupolas. Cornwall Terrace, designed by Decimus Burton under Nash's supervision, was the first terrace to be completed. The westernmost bow window, two

storeys high and supported by caryatids, is noteworthy.

12. You leave the Outer Circle through York Gate. Dividing the two mighty blocks that comprise York Terrace, this is one of Nash's grandest flourishes within the park although here, again, nothing is quite what it seems. From the park side, the view is of two great palaces, each supported by gigantic columns with a pedimented portico in the centre and a pair of large villas acting as pavilions at the easternmost end. In fact, each block contained twenty dwellings apiece but, since their entrances were in the lane to the rear, the buildings presented an uninterrupted front to the park. Return to Regent's Park Underground station along the Marylebone Road.

6. A trip on the Regent's Park Canal is a pleasant narrow-boat diversion. You pass through the Park and beside the Zoo and slip quietly past the back gardens and door of north London. The banks are a rural riverside, fringed with wild flowers and haunted by wild creatures. Herons, dabchicks and other waterfowl barely turn their heads as the boat glides by. The starting point for the trip is Camden Lock.

7. In the beginning, Nash had intended York Terrace to be

A side-trip along the Regent's Park Canal (right) provides a pleasant contrast to Nash's monumental architecture.

continuous, but, just as he was about to build, his fellow-architect Thomas Hardwick was putting the finishing touches to the new Marylebone parish church to the rear. Always quick to spot a dramatic opportunity, Nash divided the terrace in two to act as a splendid frame for the view of the church and its cupola from within the park.

Park Fact File

essential. There are lunchtime and evening bandstand concerts and occasional lakeside theatre. Boat hire facilities (rowing boats and electric launches) on the Boating Lake are open from April to September.

Opening times
The park is open from 5 a.m. until dusk.

How do you get there?
By Underground
Regent's Park, Great Portland Street, Baker Street, St John's Wood and Camden Town.

By bus
2, 13, 18, 27, 30, 74, 82, 113, 135, 139, 159, 189, 274, C2.

By car
There is parking along Chester Road towards the Inner Circle, along the Inner Circle close to The Holme and in designated areas around the Outer Circle. Note that parking is now pay-and-display and that the scheme operates on Sundays. There is a car and coach park at Gloucester Slips, close to London Zoo.

Comfort stops
There are lavatories, plus a nappy-changing room, by the Chester Gate Park Café, by the entrance to the Broad Walk, at Gloucester Green, and at the entrance to Primrose Hill. There are more lavatories to the right of York Bridge and across Longbridge. Refreshments at the Rose Park Café in Queen Mary's Gardens, Queen Mary's Gardens Park Café, Home Green Park Café across Longbridge, the Broad Walk Park Café, the Park Café at the Tennis Centre off York Bridge Road, the Chester Gate Park Café kiosk and the Park Café kiosk in the playground at Marylebone Green. All the Park Cafés have gourmet ice cream points and there are ice cream kiosks – and, in summer, ice cream tricycles – throughout the park.

For adults
The Open Air Theatre season runs from the end of May to early September. Advance booking is

For children
There are three children's playgrounds in the park, to the left of Avenue Gardens on Marylebone Green, to the left of the Outer Circle just by Parkway, and by the Boating Lake near the Park Café refreshment kiosk and opposite Hanover Island. Each of the three playgrounds is fully-equipped with sandpits, swings and the like, and has an attendant.

Other children's facilities include the children's boating pond, where rowing boats, canoes and pedalos can be hired for children over the age of 5. In summer, there are special children's events. Contact the Park Information Office for more details. Primrose Hill has its own children's play area.

Please remember
Fishing is prohibited on the park's lakes. Though dogs are welcome in the park, there are a few places (like the children's play area), where they are forbidden.

Contact points
The Park Information Office is at The Store Yard, Inner Circle, Regent's Park, London NW1 4NR, tel: 0171 486 7905. Contact this office for general information about what's on when in the park and to book sports pitches (the park has football, cricket, hockey, lacrosse, rounders and softball facilities). Visit the Park web site at www.royalparks.co.uk.

Tennis and netball courts, located near the Park Café off York Bridge Road, can be booked by telephone on 0171 724 0643. There are also softball and boules pitches on Primrose Hill. Other useful contact numbers are 0171 724 0643 for the Golf and Tennis School, 0171 486 2431/1933 for the Open Air Theatre and 0171 449 6236/6363 for London Zoo.

Pictures
By kind permission of The Royal Parks Agency. The Costume Society, London. Chris Harris/Times Newspapers Limited. Martin Jones. London Metropolitan Archives. Alistair Muir/Open Air Theatre. Dennis Sterne. Westminster City Archive. Geoffrey Young. Ready Money Fountain watercolour courtesy of Colvin and Moggridge. Photographs on pages 24 and 30 (top) by Richard Turpin from **London** by Louise Nicholson, published by Francis Lincoln. John Nash portrait reproduced by kind permission of the Principal, Fellows and Scholars of Jesus College, Oxford. Decimus Burton portrait courtesy of the National Portrait Gallery, London. All maps Courtesy of Park Café. Cover picture courtesy of Images Colour Library.